Poems from Under My Bed

LOL Halloween Rhymes

by Alan Katz

illustrated by Gary LaCoste

TRICK OR TREAT

To Benjamin Muller,
who saved our house on Halloween.

ISBN 978-0-545-48295-0

Copyright © 2013 by Alan Katz

All rights reserved. Published by Scholastic Inc.

SCHOLASTIC and associated logos are trademarks
and/or registered trademarks of Scholastic Inc.

12 11 10 9 8 7 6 5 4 3 2 1   13 14 15 16 17 18/0

Printed in the U.S.A.   40

First Scholastic printing, October 2013

Always Tell the Tooth

I sure love the treats I've collected.

I eat them from night until morn.

Though, clearly, my teeth I've neglected.

'Cause they now look like candy corn.

Orange You Glad I Wrote This?

The pumpkin it's my job to scoop.

So Mom can make us pumpkin soup.

And pumpkin pie.

And pumpkin bread.

Pumpkin muffins.

Pumpkin bed.

Pumpkin walls.

And pumpkin floor.

I don't love pumpkins

anymore.

W-W-Who's There?

There's a strange orange face in the window.

Rotted teeth,

crooked smile,

and green beard.

It makes me feel weepy.

And know what's so creepy?

That's not a pumpkin—

it's our neighbor.

How weird!

TAP
TAP

Boo (Hoo Hoo)

My ghost costume is fooling the whole town.

To all, I'm a total surprise.

But with every step I take, I trip and fall down.

(Mom didn't make holes for my eyes.)

MGLUMPH!

I've got a mouthful of candy

so large it puffs up my cheeks.

If you have any questions,

I'll just nod my head . . .

'cause I may be like this for weeks.

Knock, knock.

Whooooooo!

Three costumes means more candy.

Chew, chew, chew!

Something to Chew On . . .

Grandpa is bobbing for apples!

In the water, he digs underneath.

When he comes up for air,

I will tell him—

it'd be easier if he put in his teeth!

On Second Thought

Trick or treat!

Trick or treat!

Whoever thought of that's the worst.

Because you see,

it seems to me

the *treat* part should always come first!

That's How It Goes

A bag of goodies!

A bag of goodies!

A bag of goodies!

A bag of goodies!

A bag of goodies!

A bag of goodies!

A pile of wrappers!

From Wow . . . to Ow!

Candy is nice.

But take my advice:

I just found out,

without a doubt,

too much yum, yum, yummy

makes

giant tum, tum, tummy

aches!

gurgle

BOO!

It's "Two" Confusing

My sisters are twins

and they have the same costume.

But there's just one terrible hitch:

same hats,

same gloves,

same brooms,

same makeup . . .

so I can't tell witch one is witch.

HEE HEE HEE HEE

What a Fright!

Shriek!

Gasp!

Howl!

Oh my!

Gee whiz!

No, I didn't see a ghost—

Our teacher just gave a pop quiz!

Ta-Da! (Ha-Ha!)

Costume contest!

Oh, what fun!

The judging time has just begun!

A clown, a duck, a lamb, a shark.

A llama that glows in the dark.

More Slop! More Glop!

Making my brother's costume

was not such a very hard job.

'Cause he dressed as a messy eater

and the truth is, he's just

a big slob.

Thanks a LOT

On Halloween

in our neighborhood,

generosity abounds.

Now that's really fine,

and I don't mean to whine,

but my treat bag weighs 68 pounds!

TUG PULL

TREATS

Saving Is My Business

I'm a superhero

with a surfer mask

and bushy tail.

It's not that my family's creative.

It's just . . .

Mom bought my costume on sale.

The Perfect Deal

I think it'd be so cool

if I could be a full-time ghoul.

I think it would be the most

if I could be a full-time ghost.

I think I would never tire

of being a full-time vampire.

Now I'll stop these silly rhymes

if you'll give me candy 62 times.

COOL GHOUL

It's Up in the Air

People think I'm an astronaut.

They say I should go up to the moon.

It might be 'cause I'm an explorer.

Or 'cause I've worn this spacesuit since June.

Tricky Stuff

Today I'm a famous magician.

Just watch as things soar overhead.

A car! A boat! A scooter! A house!

Tomorrow, it's back to plain old Fred.

Wait Until Later

Well, hello, my name is Mary.

My brother thinks I'm very scary.

He said, "Your costume is as spooky as it can get!"

Only problem is—

I'm not wearing one yet!

I Wonder . . .

Do ghosts celebrate Halloween?

To them, just what does that day mean?

Do they make each other flip their lids

by dressing up as human kids?

BOO!

Do You Think I'm A-Door-Able?

Dad dressed me up as a front door.

But it's not a good costume, I fear.

'Cause people keep trying to knock on my nose

and others just twist on my ear.

Oh, why couldn't I just be a sailor?

Or a doctor?

A chef would be swell.

Hey, kid, step away—'cause I'm *not* a front door,

and please stop trying to ring my bell!

Nonstop Swap!

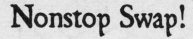

I'll trade the nuts for the raisins,

and the beans for the bran.

Then the bar for the crispy,

and the jar for the can.

Then the can for the nuts,

and the crispy for the jar.

Then the raisins for the beans

and the bran for the bar.

Somehow I think

in these deals I've been outsmarted.

'Cause after trading and trading . . .

I'm right back where I started!

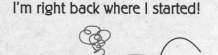

Can You Dig This?

My best friend is dressed as a groundhog.

He saw his shadow.

So what does that mean?

I think he looks great.

And the best news of all:

We get six more weeks of Halloween.

It's Pretty (Awful)

Cobwebs on the ceiling.

Cobwebs in the hall.

Cobwebs on the tables.

Cobwebs on the wall.

Cobwebs on my brother.

Cobwebs on my sis'.

We didn't decorate for Halloween.

See, we always live like this.

Please Don't Think We're Cuckoo

I'm dressed as a clock

and my sister is a bird.

Everyone's saying, "Aw, that's sweet."

And when we ring doorbells,

together we say,

Happy Halloween, and . . . tick or tweet!

I'm So Boo-Tiful!

My dad is dressed as Santa.

My brother is an elf.

I'm the Ghost of Christmas Past,

and I have to admit—

I'm awfully afraid of myself!

Go Away!

When ghost kids go on vacation

with their ghost daddies

and ghost mamas,

they sometimes go to Mali-boo

and sometimes to the Boo-hamas!

The Future Looks Delicious

Trick or treat!

I'm a fortune teller.

(It's a skill that comes in handy.)

Your future is a generous one:

You're gonna give me candy!

White and Wrong

Outside it's a winter scene.

'Cause we got snow on Halloween!

I was gonna be a ghostly fright

Till mom said, "No dressing all in white!"

You see, she would not allow me

because she thought the guy might plow me!

35

Someone Who Really (S)cares

Creaky bones

and rattling teeth!

Spooky sounds that scare my brother.

I'm not afraid

because I know

that isn't a ghost . . .

it's Grandmother!

Mayhem on the Menu

If you go to the desert

for Halloween,

you might get shakes and twitches.

'Cause flying above

and landing below

are frightfully scary sand-witches.

Color Me Haunted

Nothing rhymes with orange,

and to me, that's really freaky.

Oh, wait, perhaps there's "door hinge"—

and on Halloween, it's creaky!

CREAKK

TRICK OR TREAT

Costume Chaos

I want a costume coolish,

and something not too ghoulish.

How about a gas pump?

Or maybe a wrench?

Never mind—

They're too fuelish and toolish!

Hay Look!

My whole family's dressed up as a horse!

This costume's the fruit of Mom's labors.

As we prance about town,

everyone stops to shout,

GIDDY UP!!

I'm Not That Sweet

Dressing up like a piece of candy

can really be a drag.

My costume's so real,

while I stood at the door,

Mom dropped me into a kid's bag!

Some Thrilling News

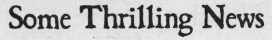

Tonight I'm a ghost

and that's special.

Which gives me a brilliant idea—

If people give candy each time I say "boo,"

I'll keep up this haunting all year!

A Halloween Howdy

Have you ever seen a cowboy goblin?

Well, take a look,

I've got one handy.

It's my big brother in a cowboy suit . . .

and look how he's goblin' candy!

Lip-Lip-Hooray!

Lemon candies, sour candies,

I'm a tart and tangy feaster!

Only problem is

I may not unpucker

at least until next Easter!

Without a Doubt . . . Watch Out!

Be safe and smart on Halloween.

Smile widely and always say thank you.

Remember your manners!

And most of all,

keep alert . . .

'cause I will surely prank you!

COUNT KATZ

Alan Katz is the author of many popular children's books, including *Take Me Out of the Bathtub and Other Silly Dilly Songs*; *Ricky Vargas: The Funniest Kid in the World*; and *OOPS!* Alan is also a six-time Emmy-nominated writer for TV series including *The Rosie O'Donnell Show*, the animated series *Taz-Mania*, Disney's *Raw Toonage* and *Goof Troop*, the Grammy Awards and Tony Awards, many Nickelodeon shows, and a lot of network specials and game shows. He has also created comic books, trading-card sets, web videos, TV commercials, and hundreds of other special projects for kids and their parents. Alan lives with his wife and four kids in Fairfield County, Connecticut.